Self-Este

Kids

- Every Parent's Greatest Gift

How To Raise Kids To Have Confidence In Themselves And Their Own Abilities

Table Of Contents

Introduction

First of all, thank you for downloading this book on self-esteem for kids. This book will help you learn how self-esteem develops in children. It will also give you step-by-step instructions for building up your child's self-esteem in a natural way. The ultimate goal of this book is to help you build and maintain your child's self-esteem, as well as help raise their self-esteem if it has fallen to an all-time low.

Many parents do not recognize the importance of self-esteem. Even if they know that it is important, they are not aware of how self-esteem develops or what they can do to help. However, the fact of the matter is that parents are the primary influence on a child's self-esteem. High self-esteem and self-confidence are the greatest gifts you can give your child.

With high self-esteem, your child will be able to succeed in school and work, but more importantly, in life in general. They will have healthy relationships, become successful in their chosen career, and be able to live productive and happy lives. Self-esteem is a necessary tool for them to have as they grow and become adults. By giving them this gift you will be giving them the most precious gift of all—a precious way for them to realize and reach their own sense of happiness.

Please keep in mind while reading this book that while every child is different, all children need these things in their lives. You know your child best, but at least most of the strategies and tips in this book will apply.

Thank you again for downloading this book. Without further ado, let's discuss self-esteem, and why it is important.

Chapter 1: Self-Esteem and Why It is Important

Great self-esteem is one of the most important gifts you will ever give your child. But what is it exactly? How do you define something so seemingly elusive?

Self-esteem simply defined is having confidence in one's self, worth and abilities. It is about self-respect. A child cannot develop self-esteem if they feel that they are worthless in any way. Likewise they cannot build self-esteem if they feel that there is nothing they are good at, or that they have no talents.

Self-esteem, in the end, is all about self-worth. What does your child think they are worth? Do they recognize how much they mean to you, and how important they are to you and the world around them? Do they understand that everyone has set backs, but everyone also has talents and abilities that increase their worth? Does your child know what these abilities and talents are?

Most of these questions would be hard to answer. It is difficult to ask these types of questions to young children. They often do not understand what you want them to say. In older children the questions are just as useless because the child will likely lie or simply refuse to answer. As a parent it is your job to judge your child's self-esteem based on actions, moods and temperaments.

Self-Esteem is Important to Kids

Many parents underestimate the impact of self-esteem on children. Children with good self-esteem often perform better in school, make advance preparations for college and career goals and are more social. They tend to succeed much easier than children with poor self-esteem.

Children with low self-esteem, however, show an even greater impact. These children become the statistics we hear almost daily. Children with low self-esteem often become depressed, even if they don't show it. In fact, children with low self-esteem are much less likely to let anyone know that something is wrong. Depression and emotional distress can lead to a number of alarming things.

Self-harm is just one of the potential outcomes for children with low self-esteem. Self-harm can be anything from cutting to anorexia (starving oneself) or bulimia (binging and purging). The number of cases of self-harm in children ages 10-17 have increased dramatically over the last ten years. While there have been few studies done to come up with hard statistics, there is no doubt that at least 1% of America's youth population practices some type of self-harm.

The most severe consequence of low self-esteem is suicide. No parent wants to contemplate that their child would ever do such a thing. However, it is vitally important to understand that this is a very real threat for kids today. It is estimated that every day an average of 5,400 youth grades 7-12 make a suicide attempt each day. That is a huge number of children that likely could have been helped long before such an attempt was ever even thought of by the child.

Improving your child's self-esteem is one of the most important ways you can prevent self-harm and suicide. Many children will decide not to commit suicide even after making the decision to do so. Their decision is often based on just one kind word, comment or action. By assuring your child daily that they have worth, you greatly limit the chance that they will resort to such drastic measures, even if they suffer from low self-esteem or depression.

The Importance of Self-Esteem Long Term

The self-esteem your child develops now will carry with them into adulthood. As your child grows to a teenager, their self-esteem becomes even more rooted and harder to change. Teens with low self-esteem generally perform poorly in school, making it difficult to gain entry to good colleges and universities. This can affect their career choices and their very lives.

Self-esteem also plays a large role in the success your child could have as an adult. Adults with low self-esteem tend to avoid jobs and career moves that would put them in the spotlight. They do not go after promotions because they feel that they are not good enough, and will not earn the promotion anyway. Low self-esteem can also lead adults to avoid all social situations, causing loneliness and depression.

As your child gets older it becomes more difficult to change their self-esteem. It is important to work to raise your child's self-esteem early so that these issues do not crop up later in life.

If you raise your child with good self-esteem, you can be secure in the fact that your child will become a productive and successful adult. There is no greater peace of mind than knowing your child can carry on when you are no longer there to hold their hand.

Chapter 2: How Self-Esteem Develops

Self-esteem develops over time. It is not something that can be rushed, and it is not something that can be held off until your child is older. Ideally the building up of self-esteem should begin occurring in the toddler years. As your child begins to develop their personality and find their way in their small world, you should be working to make sure that their self-esteem grows with them.

Think of this as a clean white board. Your child doesn't know what self-esteem is, and likely doesn't care. He or she only knows that they are trying to learn to do a million new things, and sometimes those things are hard. How you react, encourage and teach them about their world is reflected on that white board. You can either paint a beautiful picture or paint it black, like the void that will be hard to fill once created.

Self-esteem develops in different ways in different stages of childhood. It is important to understand each stage. It will help you identify the level of your child's self-esteem while in these age groups, and will give you insight into how to better build up your child's self-esteem using tools that are age appropriate.

Babies

Babies do not have a sense of self. They see themselves as a part of the parent or main caregiver. However, self-esteem can start at this early age. As babies are cared for when they need something or cry, they are being shown that they matter in the world. This is the first building blocks of self-esteem development. One of the simplest ways you can assist in this development is by talking and singing to your baby frequently throughout the day.

Toddlers

Toddlers are becoming more aware of themselves, but still do not have a true sense of self. Between the ages of 1 and 3 your child will grow and develop at a rapid pace. Part of this development is discovering a sense of self as a definite personality emerges. This is truly the beginning of the development of self-esteem.

Toddlers need to be encouraged and praised often. They need to know when they are good at something. They also need to know that it is okay to make mistakes as they learn, and that it doesn't take away from their self-worth. You should tell a toddler how much you love them and are proud of them, even at random moments when they haven't done something to please you.

Ages 3-5

This is perhaps the most impressionable age. By age 3 children have discovered who they are, and are beginning to have a real sense of self-worth. How you react to your child during these important years will shape their self-esteem for the rest of their lives.

At this point in their development children will begin to compare themselves with others. As they venture out into the world and spend time with other children they will begin to see that some are taller, some are thinner and some are smarter or more talented. All of this will help shape how your child sees themselves.

It is important that through this process you talk to your child about the children they see and their own abilities and talents. Bring it up in idle conversation, and present opportunities to make them feel special for who they are. This will help build good self-esteem, especially when it comes to areas that make your child feel self-conscious.

Ages 5-10

If you are watchful, this is the time when you will begin to see if your child is developing low self-esteem. Children of this age should be making friends and becoming social.

Children just starting out in school have some pressure to learn the rules and get used to the schoolwork, but should still feel as though they can succeed. If your child is failing in school or doesn't seem to be picking up on simple concepts, talk to them about whether or not they feel they can do it. Encourage them and let them know that they can do it, given practice. They should know that even if they need help they are succeeding by simply asking for it.

As your child continues through school the stress generally lessens as they get used to the routine. Children at this stage usually develop great self-esteem by learning new things, getting good grades, and spending time with friends, family and teachers who truly care about them.

Pre-Teens

The ages of 10 to 12 are among the hardest for a child to endure. No longer feeling like a child but not quite a teenager getting ready to be an adult, these children have a hard time figuring out where they fit in. This is where the building of self-esteem is tested. If your child has a good foundation for self-esteem they will probably get through this confusing period of life with few problems. If, however, your child does not have a solid foundation you will see it immediately as problems surface. This is generally the period of time when your child's self-esteem is set, usually for the rest of their lives.

Teens

As a teenager your child's self-esteem becomes even more solidified. It can alter somewhat in this stage due to the pressures of high school, social pressures most of all. The need to fit in and the need for social interaction can greatly affect self-esteem. However, if your child has good foundations for self-esteem that have survived the pre-teen years, your child will likely thrive in high school and go on to become a very confident and productive adult.

Chapter 3: Do's and Don'ts of Building Self-Esteem

As your child learns and grows, it is important that you help build up their self-esteem on a daily basis. There are a lot of things you can do to give your child this precious gift. On the other hand, there are also a lot of mistakes that parents often make that can tear down a child's self-esteem and make it more difficult for them to develop.

Knowing what you should and should not do may come easily for some parents. Other parents may not realize the damage their actions and words are doing to their child's self-esteem. Ideally parents will learn these differences while their children are still at a young age. However, it is never too late to start helping your child develop their self-esteem.

Do's of Building Self-Esteem

Give Your Child a Sense of Future Success

Talk to your child often about their plans for the future. These will change constantly as your child grows, but it is important to get them thinking about what successes they may have in the short term and long term future. As they tell you what they want to be when they grow up, talk to them about what is needed to achieve their goals, and let them know that they have what it takes to be successful. You can start talking about the future with your child as early as age 2, although at that point the talks will likely be more about school than future careers.

Give Your Child a Sense of Belonging

You and other family members should consistently give your child affection, and let them know that they belong in your family. It will also help for younger children to be part of a playgroup or preschool. This will help them establish a feeling of belonging to a group. As your child gets older, consider putting them in at least one club or extracurricular activity to give them an additional sense of belonging. If done early, by the time your child reaches high school they will feel that they belong to a certain group, which will make it easier for them to maintain self-esteem in that environment.

Give Your Child a Sense of Purpose and Responsibility

Children need to feel that they have a reason for being. While open play is important and encouraged, children at all ages need to have a purpose. It can help to give children a goal, such as learning a new skill. As your child gets older you can also assign them chores and allow them to assist you in tasks and projects. Even a two year old can help clean their own room. This will give them something to take pride in, an accomplishment that they can feel good about.

Praise Your Child Often

Letting your child know when they have done something good not only teaches them right from wrong, but it also boosts their self-esteem in a big way. When you praise your child they will know that they are good at something. You should even praise your child when they make some mistakes. Praise them for their effort and for the way they handled the outcome of their actions. This will let them know that it is okay to make mistakes, and that it is not a reflection of who they are as a person.

Allow Your Child to Make Choices

Allowing your child to make choices will give them some control over their own small world. As their choices lead to good outcomes they will learn to have confidence in themselves, boosting their self-esteem. Choices should be age appropriate and limited at first. This will ensure a good outcome regardless of the choice made. As children get older they can be presented with more choices, each with their own outcomes. If a choice leads to a poor outcome, it is important that you talk with your child and make sure they understand that bad choices do not make them a bad person.

Give Your Child Daily Encouragement

Encouragement and praise are often used interchangeably, but they are actually very different things. Praise is when you tell your child how good they have done, or how proud of them you are for an accomplishment. Encouragement is when you tell your child you know they can do something, and urge them to give it a try. When your child expresses an interest in art, encourage them to pursue it by telling them you know they are talented and can be a success. Giving a child encouragement lets them know that you think they can do it, and it boosts their confidence in their abilities as well as their self-esteem.

Give Your Child Respect

Talk to your child the way you would expect to be talked to. Listen to them regardless of the topic of conversation. Show them that you respect their opinion and understand what they are saying. This does not mean that you have to agree with them. But you should express your disagreement in a calm and respectful way. Treat them with the utmost respect at all times. This teaches them to be respectful to others, while also showing them that you see them as an individual, not just your child.

Don'ts for Parents

Never Associate a Bad Choice or Mistake with the Child's Personality

Telling a child that they are a "bad boy" when they do something wrong is only going to lower their self-esteem. When you say such things you are telling them that their behavior makes them a bad person. This is not the case. The emphasis should be placed on the action being bad, even though the child themselves are not bad. This is an important distinction to make in the way you talk to your child and in the way they understand you.

Constant Nagging

It is one thing to tell your child that they need to clean their room, or occasionally remind them to sit up straight. However, when you constantly nag your child about small things it makes them feel as though nothing they do is good enough. They begin to feel that this reflects on them as a person, and that they are not good enough for you. This is a common method of destruction for self-esteem. You may feel that you are simply trying to teach your child, but there are limits.

Avoid Negative "You Are" Statements

If your child fails to do their chore, don't tell them that they are lazy. Tell them that it is a lazy thing to do. Making statements such as you are untidy, naughty, etc. associates the problem with the child in a negative way. Let the child know that what they are doing is wrong, but without giving them negative connotations.

Never Call Your Child Names

Even if you feel you are just giving them a hard time or playing around, you should never call your child names. Never call your child stupid, idiot, or any other names that can be much worse. When you call your child names it makes them feel that they are unloved, and that they are not worthy of being loved.

Comparing With Others

Try to avoid comparing your child with siblings or other children that they know. When you compare children against each other, it makes the child feel that they are not as good as the other child. Never tell your child "I wish you were more like your brother/sister/friend." This is detrimental to their self-esteem, and if heard often can cause serious emotional harm.

Don't Act Like They are a Burden

You should never tell your child that you wish you could go out, but they are keeping you from it because you can't get a sitter. Don't tell them that they are preventing you from working, going to school, or any other goal of yours. If your child comes to you to ask you a question or talk to you about something, don't sigh and/or roll your eyes, or flat out ignore them. These actions and words give your child the message that you would be better off without them, and that they have no worth. They will not build any self-esteem if they feel this way.

Chapter 4: Warning Signs of Low Self-Esteem

You should become well aware of the warning signs of low self-esteem early in your child's life. It is important that you take note of these signs as early as possible. The older your child becomes the harder it will be to bring up their self-esteem if it is already taken down too low.

It may seem unnecessary, but you should keep these warning signs in mind at all times. Keep a close eye on your child, and notice if they have any of these signs repetitively. Occasionally you may want to sit down and really assess your child's development and behavior to help you see possible patterns that may point to an ongoing problem.

Every child is different, and only you know your child best. It is possible that some of these behaviors are normal for your child, and do not reflect on their self-esteem level. However, this is a good guideline to use for most children.

Having just one warning sign, or only exhibiting the sign occasionally, is likely not enough to go on to determine low self-esteem. However, if your child has more than one sign and exhibits them frequently, there is definitely a problem that should be addressed.

If you are unsure if your child has any of these warning signs, you should discuss it with your co-parent or with your child's doctor. It is important to catch these signs early so that problems can be headed off before they begin to cause more complex mental health issues.

Unwillingness to Try New Things

Children who are afraid of failure due to low self-esteem will not want to try anything new. They will rebel against learning new skills or tasks. They may also refuse to take on a particular challenge, especially if it is similar to something they have failed in before. This can even extend to school, where they may feel that they are going to fail so they don't even try to do the work.

Introverted, Little Social Contact

Children who believe that they are not good enough tend to shy away from social interactions. They may want to spend more time alone in their room. They are not likely to have many friends, and will probably spend little time with the friends they do have. This should be taken as a sure warning sign of low self-esteem if your child was previously outgoing but has become withdrawn.

Self-critical Comments

This is the easiest warning sign to spot. Do not dismiss it if your child is typically saying things such as "I'm stupid" or "I never do anything right." Comments such as these made on a frequent basis are telling you outright that your child has low self-esteem. Some parents think that all teens go through this phase, and they don't take it seriously. However, in preteens and teens especially, comments such as these should not be taken lightly. Consider them a cry for help.

Difficulty Accepting Feedback

If your child tends to shy away from accepting a compliment, they probably feel that they don't deserve it. If your child gets angry or withdrawn any time they receive criticism, they likely feel that it is nothing they didn't already suspect, and it just adds to their feeling of low self-esteem. Most children who have low self-esteem cannot accept any feedback, positive or negative.

Over-exaggerating Setbacks

Children with low self-esteem feel that every setback, mistake or failure is the end of the world. Even if it is only temporary, such as making a mistake while learning a new type of math problem, to the child it is a lasting failure. Once the temporary setback has occurred, they will become very upset and agitated. They will also probably become angry or despondent when asked to attempt the problem again.

Excessive Pessimism

Low self-esteem causes a child to believe that nothing can go right, ever, at any time, as long as they are involved. This leads to a very pessimistic attitude that will carry over into every aspect of their lives. They will believe that they will not do well on a test, will not be able to participate in a discussion in class, or not be able to get a job. Younger children will act out with inappropriate behavior or anger, insisting that something will go wrong.

Perfectionism

This term is often misunderstood. Being a perfectionist does not mean that everything is always perfect. It means that if it is not perfect, the perfectionist is unhappy, even distraught. A younger child who is a perfectionist can become uncontrollably upset, throwing temper tantrums or crying without accepting a parents attempt to console them. Older children and teens are likely to become extremely angry or just plain give up on things when they are not perfect.

Refusing to Make Decisions

Low self-esteem makes you feel like you cannot be trusted to make good choices. If your child always defers to you and makes you make all of the decisions in their lives, no matter how small, this is a big signal that your child has low self-esteem. Teens who refuse to make their own decisions are especially concerning.

Constantly Attention Seeking

Children with low self-esteem really don't like feeling that way. They want to feel that they are good enough to be accepted. Younger children will demand your attention, more than is normal for their age. Preteens may cling as if they were much younger than their age, and want more attention than is warranted. For teens this type of behavior can be even more disturbing. Many teens seek attention from the opposite sex or from friends, rather than from family. This can lead to promiscuity, being in abusive relationships, or doing things (like skipping class, smoking, drinking) just to try to gain the acceptance of their peers.

Outrageous Jealousy

Some jealousy in children is normal. For example, if a child has a brand new game system and his parents can afford things you can't, it is natural for your child to be a bit jealous. However, obsessive jealousy is something that should never occur in healthy children. If your child is outrageously jealous of other children, or obsessively jealous of one child in particular, your child is likely suffering from low self-esteem. This can, however, be a sign of a more serious mental health issue as well.

Excessive Shyness

Some children are just shy by nature. You know your child best, and if this is a trait your child has had from the beginning it is likely normal for your child. However, if the shyness develops over time or seems out of character for your child, it can be an indicator of low self-esteem. Children with low self-esteem do not want to meet or get to know new people because they are afraid that those people will see them for who they believe they are, and therefore not accept them fully.

Chapter 5: Proven Strategies for Raising Self-Esteem

The building of self-esteem naturally throughout your child's development is important. But what happens when your child develops low self-esteem? You should take immediate action as soon as any warning signs are seen.

While the tips listed in the previous chapters for building self-esteem still apply, there are some additional strategies you will need to put into place to rebuild low self-esteem. It is much harder to raise low self-esteem than it is to build it up in the course of normal development.

Remember throughout this process that the goal is to provide your child with the gift of confidence and self-empowerment. Do not become frustrated, and certainly do not show your frustration to your child. Always be positive throughout this process, even when the going gets tough. These strategies will help you stay positive, and give your child a positive outlook.

Get Them to Talk About It

From a young age you should teach your children to talk about their feelings. Whether you have tried to do this or not, it may be difficult to get your child to talk about how they feel about themselves. However, it is very important that you make the attempt to talk to your child about their self-esteem.

Of course, conversations should be age appropriate. The word self-esteem should not actually be used in the conversation. It may also take more than one attempt to try to understand why your child feels the way they do. Ask questions that will prompt them to talk about themselves and their feelings, without pushing or leading them into it. Take the opportunity to talk to your child during moments when they are displaying low self-esteem. However, you can also talk to your child randomly during the course of the day.

In any conversation with your child about feelings you should not prompt them with "are you feeling sad, etc." Give them the chance to put words to their thoughts and feelings. In addition, you should never tell your child that they shouldn't feel the way they do, or that their feelings are wrong. Instead, ask them why they feel that way, and give them the reasons that you believe they are better than they feel they are.

When Your Child Says They Can't Do Something

Ask your child why they feel they can't perform the task or take on the challenge. If they don't give a reason straightaway, you can probe a bit further. Let them know that you think they can do it, and give them reasons for your belief (they are smart, they have the basic skills for the challenge). Follow up by asking your child what is difficult about the task or challenge. If they simply do not have the confidence to try, this will come out in the course of conversation. It is then your job to explain to them why they can do it, and convince them to try. When they are successful, and when given your confidence in their ability, the experience will be a self-esteem boost.

When Your Child Says They Aren't Good Enough

Many children with low self-esteem will claim that they are not good enough for many things. They may believe they are not good enough to play a sport, continue in studies with an instrument or other talent, or succeed in school. They may say that they are not good enough to hang out with someone. Whatever the situation, as soon as your child says they aren't good enough you need to ask them why. Why do you feel you are not good enough? Regardless of the answer, encourage them and let them know that they are always good enough. Give them reasons for your belief.

When Your Child Withdraws

If your child suddenly stops hanging out with friends, ask them why they do not want to spend time with them. They may give surprising answers. Often children will put the blame on the friend so that they don't have to talk about how they really feel. Hopefully you are familiar enough with their friends to know whether or not the reasons are likely or made up. If the reasons given do not seem in line with the personality or history of the friend, point this out to your child. Do not tell them that they are wrong, but instead say something like "I don't think that he meant to do that." Allow the conversation to run its course. In most cases eventually the truth about the matter will come out.

Countering Negativity

Low self-esteem always leads to a negative attitude about self and life in general. This negativity can feed upon itself to the point where your child is despondent or constantly lashing out. It is important that you do not allow this negativity to have free reign.

The easiest way to combat negativity is to counter it with positivity. However, even this can be easier said than done. Most children will not be able to do this on their own, and will depend on you to do it for them.

When Young Children Have a Negative Response

A negative response to a situation could be something blatant such as "I can't do that" or "I'm not good enough" to a much more subtle attitude of not wanting to do it. Your child could also become uncontrollable, throwing temper tantrums. Whenever your child has a negative response, try to put a positive spin on the situation. If you cannot come up with something positive about the situation, steer the conversation or train of thought of the child to another topic that is positive. Once the child is in a better mood and more reasonable you can readdress the issue that brought on the negativity.

Training Preteens and Teens to Curb Negativity

Older children, preteens and teens can be taught to combat negativity on their own. Teaching them to turn away from negative thoughts about themselves and their lives will serve them well in their adult lives. It is not something that is easy or happens immediately. It takes time and practice, and the constant reminders from you, their parent.

Start by countering your child's negative statements with positive statements. If they say, "I can't do this" say "Yes, I know you can." If they say "I'm not good enough" say "Yes you are, and this is why." As you continue in this fashion, tell your child that they can counter negativity on their own in this fashion.

When your child thinks to themselves "I'm not good enough" they can counter that negative thought with a positive one such as "I'm awesome." While they may not truly believe that they are awesome quite yet, they will begin to feel better about themselves over time. Each time they have a negative thought, they should come up with a thought that is completely the opposite and makes a positive impression.

Most preteens and teens will think that this exercise is "stupid" and may tell you that they won't do it. And, in all actuality, you won't know if they are doing it or not. You can tell them that if they say a negative comment they have to say something positive. But as far as what is going on in their own minds, you are going to be clueless. However, if you are diligent and keep reminding them of the exercise, it may begin to sink in and they could find themselves doing it without even thinking about it. When this begins to happen, low self-esteem will become a thing of the past. Don't expect immediate results from this exercise. It will take quite some time before you see a complete turnaround in their attitude.

The Power of Mindful Thinking and Action

One way for a child to counter negativity is through mindful thinking or action. You can easily teach your child to do this, and it will help stop them from thinking negative thoughts about themselves.

Cognitive behavioral therapy is a technique used by therapists for many mental health problems including depression, bipolar disorder, personality disorders, and attention deficit disorder. However, you can also use this technique to combat negative thinking. You don't need a therapist to use this technique. It is really very simple, and if you are interested in learning more than can be covered here there are a number of books available on the subject.

The principle behind cognitive behavioral therapy is to keep your mind on your task. You do not allow yourself to think about anything other than what you are doing in that moment. This can be applied a number of ways.

If your daughter has low self-esteem due to her appearance, have her brush her hair and fix her makeup mindfully. This means that she will only think about what she is doing, not what she sees (or thinks she sees) in the mirror. If your child has feelings of low self-esteem, making them think they are not capable of doing schoolwork or taking on a challenge, tell them to focus their thoughts only on the task at hand. They should not allow their minds to wander, but only focus on exactly what they are doing in the moment.

Negative thinking can be combated in this way no matter what the child is doing or where they are. They can even focus only on walking, thinking about each step as it is taken. It takes time to train the mind to work this way. Your child's mind will automatically wander to those negative thoughts. The key is to help your child understand that these thoughts do not need to rule them. They can control them by focusing on what they are doing, and doing it mindfully.

Addressing Outside Factors

Even if you have been diligent in building up your child's self-esteem, they could suffer from low self-esteem. Your efforts to bring it up at home may not be enough if there are outside influences causing the self-esteem issues.

There are many outside influences that may be affecting your child's self-esteem. Because children tend to blame themselves for these issues they are reluctant to mention it or talk about it. If you can get them to talk about their feelings and what is causing them as discussed earlier in this chapter, it will be much easier to face these influences head on. However, you may have to do a bit of digging to discover whether or not any of these issues apply to your child.

<u>Bullying</u>

Being bullied is the most common factor in a child's low self-esteem. If your child will not talk to you about what goes on at school and you suspect that they may be being bullied, you need to take matters into your own hands. Talk to the school counselor, principal and teachers. Especially in the case that you are a working parent, these individuals spend more time with your child than you do. They will have valuable insight into what is causing your child's low self-esteem. If they are being bullied, these school contacts will know about it.

Once you know the bullying is going on, you need to take action to put a stop to it. Most schools now have a zero tolerance policy, meaning that if a child is bullying someone they are immediately disciplined. If the behavior continues, the child will be suspended or expelled. However, the bullying has to be reported for it to make a difference.

Talk to your child about the situation. Let them know that you heard from their teachers that they might be bullied at school. Let them know that bullying is not their fault, and that there is something to be done about it. Encourage them to tell a teacher or the principal if bullying occurs. Your child may be frightened to do this, fearing retaliation from the bully. However, if you can get the school to back you up and let your child know that they will put a stop to the bullying, it will make a huge difference.

If your child's school is not willing to do anything about the situation, or if their policies prevent them from disciplining the bully fully, you will need to take additional action. You may need to contact the school board or attend a school board meeting to get results. If you still can't get the bullying to stop, you may need to consider moving, changing schools, or homeschooling.

Negative Teachers

It is unfortunate, but it sometimes happens that teachers contribute to low self-esteem. If your child's teacher tells them that they aren't capable, or that they are stupid or ignorant, it will do a great deal to lower their self-esteem. Children are brought up to respect authority, and teachers are definitely an authority. If the teacher is telling them that they are stupid, it must be true, right? Wrong.

Again, your child may not be willing to talk about this. They may feel ashamed that their teacher thinks this way about them. One way to tell if your child's teacher is being negative is to talk to them. Attending parent-teacher conferences can give you a clear idea of the personality of the teacher and their faith, or disbelief, in your child's abilities. You can also talk to your child's friends and ask them if the teacher is mean to your child.

If you have a teacher being negative to your child you should take immediate action. Talk to the principal first, and let him know your concerns. Demand that disciplinary action be taken. If none is taken, or if the problem continues after action, demand that the teacher be removed from the school. At the very least, your child should be switched to a different class and a different teacher. If you can't get results, go to the school board and demand action.

Negative Comments from Peers

Teenagers especially will have this problem. Teens can be mean. They will call someone too fat, too thin, ugly or plain. They will tell them that they have no fashion sense, that they are a geek, or that they are unacceptable in some other way.

Teens really take these negative comments to heart. If they hear them often enough, they will begin to believe them, and their self-esteem will plummet. While you can't do anything about what children say to your teen while at school or extracurricular activities, you can influence your child to ignore this negativity. If your child is overweight, talk to them about this. If their weight problem is due to health problems, make sure they understand that it is not their fault. If something can be done about their weight, make a plan with them for diet and exercise. You should also make sure that they don't blame themselves for their weight issue.

The key to any negative comments like this is to make sure your child understands that their appearance is not a reflection of who they are as a person. If the negative comments are about their personality or abilities, tell your child that it is okay to march to the beat of your own drum. They should never feel ashamed of who they are. And, they should know that the opinion of others should never matter to them.

The Most Important Fifteen Minutes of the Day

Set aside fifteen minutes every day. It can be in the morning over breakfast, in the evening before bed, or in the afternoon when everyone gets home. Spend that fifteen minutes with your child, just the two of you, in a quiet room with no distractions like TV or computers.

Take this time to ask your child about their day, what they have planned or what they did. Take advantage of every opportunity to let them know how special they are to you, and how much you believe in them. Then, make your child tell you ten positive things about themselves. If their self-esteem is really low it could take a while for them to come up with ten things on their own. If they get stuck and can't come up with anything, help them out by giving them a few things you know about them that are positive.

Taking this short time with your child will make a huge difference in their self-esteem. It is easy to get busy with life. When you work a full time job and your child is in school and extracurricular activities it is hard to make time to spend just talking. Taking these fifteen minutes to give your child your undivided attention will help them know how much you care about them, and it will reinforce positivity.

Even though you will only be talking for a short time, they will continue to think about the conversation and will come to look forward to your time together. As your child becomes more comfortable chatting with you in this relaxed fashion, your conversations will likely go on much longer than fifteen minutes, but this is exactly what you want. It will not only boost their self-esteem, it will help you form a closer bond with your child. This is something that is difficult, especially with preteens and teenagers.

Chapter 6: When the Going Gets Tough

Despite your best efforts, your child may still have low self-esteem. There comes a point when you must recognize that your child's problems are beyond what you can control or influence. When this happens, you should not give up.

When to Say Enough is Enough

If your child shows signs of depression, is caught harming themselves or makes a threat to harm themselves, you will need to take action. If your child is completely unresponsive to your efforts, refuses to talk to you about their problems or at all, and continues to become more and more depressed, you must try something else.

Younger children tend to respond better than older children and teens. If your child is responding to your efforts even a little bit, and are not overly depressed, you may still have time to work with them yourself. However, if you have a preteen or teenager that simply refuse to work with you, won't talk to you or open up about their feelings and problems, and won't share with you what is causing their feelings, you will need to find someone who can bring these things to light.

Why Therapy Works

If you haven't been able to help raise your child's self-esteem and you need outside help, a good therapist is the way to go. You may wonder how a stranger can succeed where you could not. There are a few different reasons that therapy works with children to raise their self-esteem.

Strangers Are...Well...Strangers

You may feel that because you are close to your child you are the best person to help them. However, it is typically much easier for a child to open up to a complete stranger than to friends and family. Part of this is that they are always afraid of what those close to them will think about them. The opinion of a stranger that they see infrequently doesn't matter nearly as much.

Another reason it helps for them to talk to a stranger is that the stranger is outside the situation. You give this person information about your child, their history and what has been going on in their lives. You tell the therapist why your child is there. Your child will also tell the therapist why they are there, if they are cooperating.

However, beyond this basic information the stranger is completely clueless. He or she must work with your child to discover what they think and feel. They can then take this learned information and make observations that are completely impartial.

While you will know your child better than the therapist, you are biased toward your child. You will also want to protect your child and only hope to make them feel better. The therapist doesn't have this attachment, and so can be more honest and straightforward with your child to help them overcome their low self-esteem.

The Therapist is Experienced in Many Techniques

There are a lot of things a therapist can do with your child to help them overcome their low self-esteem. While you can try many things at home, a therapist will have experience with many more techniques that cannot be found in books. It is also easier for the therapist to implement these techniques than for you to do it yourself simply because they have the experience of using these techniques with children and adults of all ages.

Don't Be Afraid of Therapy for Your Child

Therapy may seem a drastic step to take. However, if your own efforts are not making a difference you have to recognize that someone else may have better luck. These are trained professionals with experience in dealing with self-esteem issues, and the problems that can arise from them.

You should not feel as though you are a bad parent just because your child needs therapy. Sometimes children need this type of help, and it is not the fault of the parents. For some children it is simply easier to talk to someone outside the situation, someone removed from their everyday lives.

You should also not feel that therapy is only for seriously disturbed children. Many children benefit from therapy without having any serious mental health issues. Therapy is not the same thing as psychiatric treatment. It is simply someone familiar with their problems helping them address those problems in a productive way.

Convincing Your Child to Go to Therapy

Once you have convinced yourself of the need for therapy, you will need to convince your child. This may be even more difficult than making the decision to send them to therapy in the first place.

Of course, you could just make them go. You are, after all, their parent. You can tell them that they are going, whether they like it or not. You can threaten them with grounding if they don't go. But this does nothing to serve your purpose. Such threats and absolutes without reasons only serve to further lower their self-esteem, and can even destroy their trust in you.

Take a completely different approach. Sit down with your child for a heart to heart talk. Let them know that you know they are unhappy, and you want to help them become happier with their life. Tell your child that even though you have not been able to help them yourself, there is someone who can help them. They will probably object to the therapy at first, and may continue to object until they have been to see the therapist a few times. However, if you are honest with your child and convince them to give it a try as a favor to you, you will be much more successful in getting them to go.

However, you still need to be firm. Let your child know that this is for their own good, and it is something that needs to be done. If they begin talking to you about their problems and wanting you to help them yourself, this can be a great opportunity. You may want to give that option another try before starting therapy. However, if they do not open up but simply argue the point, you should not give in. This is something that must be done for them to be happy, productive children, teens and adults.

Finding Potential Therapists

There are many ways to go about finding a suitable therapist. While you can certainly go to the Internet or yellow pages and find many therapists in your area, this is typically not the best way to find one that will help your child. Instead, you should look for answers through more reliable means. You have many sources at your fingertips that will assist you in getting the help you need for your child.

School Counselor

The school counselor may be able to talk to your child about their self-esteem issues or any other problems they may be having. However, because the counselor is a school official your child may likely rebel and refuse to talk to them, much the same way they won't talk to you.

However, that doesn't mean that your child's school counselor can't help. In fact, the counselor will probably be able to refer you to many therapists that are known to work with children of the same age. They may have intimate knowledge of at least one of the therapists they can refer you to, and will likely know which ones are the best for self-esteem issues.

Family Doctor or Pediatrician

Your family doctor or child's pediatrician should have some resources for you if you just ask. Let your child's doctor know about your concerns, and ask them if they can refer you to someone who can help. If they don't know of a therapist personally their office should still be able to refer you to a partnering therapy clinic.

Insurance

Many people do not realize that there are very good referral networks with their health insurance company. Most insurance companies have a specific number to call just for mental health issues. You can call this number and be referred to therapists that your insurance covers. However, the database that the insurance company uses may not give them information such as what age groups the therapist works with, or what their specialty is.

County Health Department

If you do not have insurance it is harder to find a therapist. You will need to find one that will work with you on payments, hopefully working on a sliding scale for the fee. If there is no therapist available with a sliding scaled fee, you can usually find one that gives a discount for self-pay customers.

The best way to find therapists with this special requirement is to contact your county health department. It is their job to be able to refer you to the places where you can get care with or without insurance, and this includes mental health. Some counties will offer health and mental health services through the health department for those without insurance. Other counties have organizations that help people in your situation, and while they are not directly connected to the health department, they are connected to them through referrals.

Choosing a Therapist

When you choose a therapist you will need to take several factors into consideration. You want to make sure that the therapist you choose is the best person to help your child. This is difficult to determine based on a name and a referral. You should always interview a potential therapist before making an appointment. Talk to them over the phone at length. Give them a brief description of your concerns and why you want the appointment, and then ask them a series of questions to determine who is the most suitable therapist for your child.

What Age Group Does the Therapist Generally Work With?

It is important that the therapist you choose is familiar with working with children of the same age as your child. A therapist that typically works with adults will not have the ability to put themselves on your child's level, which must be done to gain their trust and get them to open up and follow therapeutic techniques. A therapist that typically works with young children will not be appropriate for a teenager, because they will be used to lowering themselves much lower than is necessary for a teen. Preteens also need their own specialized form of therapy.

What Techniques Does the Therapist Use?

Most therapists will mention cognitive behavioral therapy as one of their techniques. Even if you have tried this at home it is well worth allowing the therapist to try it again. The therapist has a lot more experience than you do with this type of therapy, and may have more success with it than you did alone.

The therapist may also mention things like goal setting, focusing on solutions to problems and coming up with activities that the child can be successful in to boost confidence and self-esteem. They may also have more creative techniques to try, as well as the ability to simply talk to your child and listen to them, giving them guidance and sympathy that is difficult for them to take from friends and family.

At What Point will the Therapist Tell You What is Going On?

It is important that you know what is going on with your child. If you have been unsuccessful with getting your child to open up to you to discuss their problems, it is even more important that the therapist keeps you informed. However, there is a greater need for the child to feel that they can trust the therapist.

Most therapists will tell you that they are not going to tell you anything that is said in the session with your child without your child's permission. This develops a sense of trust with the therapist, and helps the child open up more fully to completely address all problems with ease. However, there should be exceptions.

If your child talks about hurting others, being hurt by someone, or hurting themselves, the therapist should immediately tell you what is going on, with or without the child's permission. This includes if your child is being bullied at school, if they are thinking about harming themselves in some fashion, or if they feel that they might be violent towards others, even if they have not actually taken any of these actions.

The therapist you choose should also assure you that they will do their best to get your child to agree to tell you about their sessions. The therapist should not want to keep you in the dark. However, that patient/doctor confidentiality is still important, even with minors.

The Last Resort

If your child does not respond to therapy, you may need to take more drastic action. If your child become harmful to others or themselves, or if they fall into a deep depression, you will need to do something more. More intensive therapy may be required. In addition, your child may need to see a psychiatrist and be put on medications for depression and/or anxiety. Do not be afraid to turn to these resources if necessary. They are not a permanent solution, but they will help your child become healthier and happier when nothing else will work.

Conclusion

In the end, your child should be as happy and healthy as humanly possible. As parents we all want this for our children. When you take their happiness seriously and wish the best for them, they cannot help but to succeed in life.

High self-esteem is the greatest gift you will ever give your child. Without self-esteem and self-confidence, your child will not grow to be a productive adult. With this precious gift ingrained into their being, they will be able to work toward the career of their dreams, be in healthy relationships, and will eventually grow up to be wonderful parents themselves one day.

I hope this book helped you learn some new strategies for building up your child's self-esteem from an early age. If you are getting a late start, I hope that this book has helped give you a new outlook on this area of your child's health and well-being. If you are at your wits end, and do not know where else to turn, I hope this book has given you the strategies and resources to help your child no matter how low their self-esteem as dropped.

Finally, I would love to hear how this book has helped you, so if you liked this book I would really appreciate it if you'd leave a review and tell me all about it. You can leave a review by searching for the title of this book on www.amazon.com.

Bonus: Preview Of "Minimalism: How To Declutter, De-Stress and Simplify Your Life With Simple Living"

Today, a growing number of people are becoming dissatisfied with their lives and turning to simpler ways of working, living and raising their children. This book will explore the philosophy of minimalism and how it can streamline your life, declutter your home, reduce stress and reconnect you to what's truly important.

You'll find ways to adopt a mindset that promotes simplicity and elegance in your every day life, and rethink your dependence on material possessions. Whether in our wardrobes, kitchens, work lives or our deeper sense of personal and spiritual purpose, we could all do with focusing on things that align with our values and reducing the distraction of those things that pull us away from them. This book shows you how.

For those born and raised in the height of our consumer society, the idea that happiness and personal fulfillment is found in *stuff* is more or less a given. The capitalist machine we all live within requires only one thing of us: that we should constantly want, and the things we should want are to be found, usually, in malls. Malls that are filled with strategically placed advertising, with the sole purpose to entice and lure you, trying to convince you that you need, not want, their specific product. Our economy relies heavily on a steady stream of consumption: better clothes, cars, bigger houses and things to fill those houses with, the newest appliances, Christmas decorations, pet toys, jewelry, office furniture, pot plants, gaming consoles, specialty tires, luxury soaps... the array of stuff is simply dazzling.

But if you are reading this there's a chance you find this overabundance just a little... exhausting. Paradoxically, there seems to be a sad sort of emptiness in filling up one's life with more things. What is simple and truly valuable often seems to be completely hidden under mountains of what is unnecessary. Although advertising tells us the best way to solve problems is to *buy* solutions, tranquility and a graceful life seem to elude us, no matter what we buy or how much of it.

Minimalism is an aesthetic, a philosophy and a way of life. This book takes a look at how deeply liberating a simpler life can be, and shows you ways you can adopt a calmer, more deliberate way of living and working. Minimalism is about clearing away the clutter that is distracting from what is really important. It's about rethinking our attitudes to ownership, to our lifestyles and to our innermost values.

This book will give practical advice on owning fewer clothes, de-cluttering your life, simplifying your daily routine and reducing mindless consumerism. It will also explore how practical changes to our surroundings can lead to a previously unknown inner peace and calm.

Other Books By This Author:

- Minimalism: How To Declutter, De-Stress And Simplify Your Life With Simple Living

- The Minimalist Budget: A Practical Guide On How To Save Money, Spend Less And Live More With A Minimalist Lifestyle

- How To Stop Worrying and Start Living – What Other People Think Of Me Is None Of My Business: Learn Stress Management and How To Overcome Relationship Jealousy, Social Anxiety and Stop Being Insecure

- Mindful Eating: A Healthy, Balanced and Compassionate Way To Stop Overeating, How To Lose Weight and Get a Real Taste of Life by Eating Mindfully

Printed in Great Britain
by Amazon.co.uk, Ltd.,
Marston Gate.